VISIONAIRE'S FASHION 2000
Designers at the Turn of the Millennium

LAURENCE KING

USAGERS
Aidez-nous à tenir
l'établissement propre

Popy Moreni vs. Azzedine Alaïa
Photographed by Jean-Paul Goude

SALLE ANNEXE Nº2

W/D
17/10/19

ART AND DESIGN: FLORENTINO J. PAMINTUAN, GREGORY FOLEY
PRODUCTION MANAGER: JAKE McCABE
PROJECT COORDINATOR: JORGE GARCIA

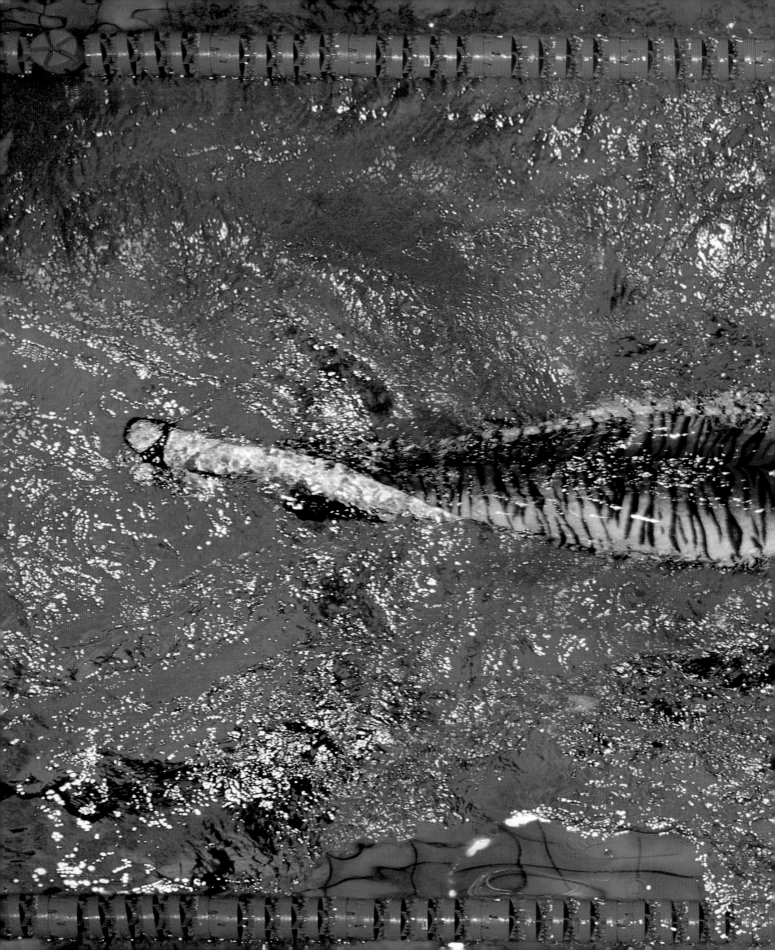

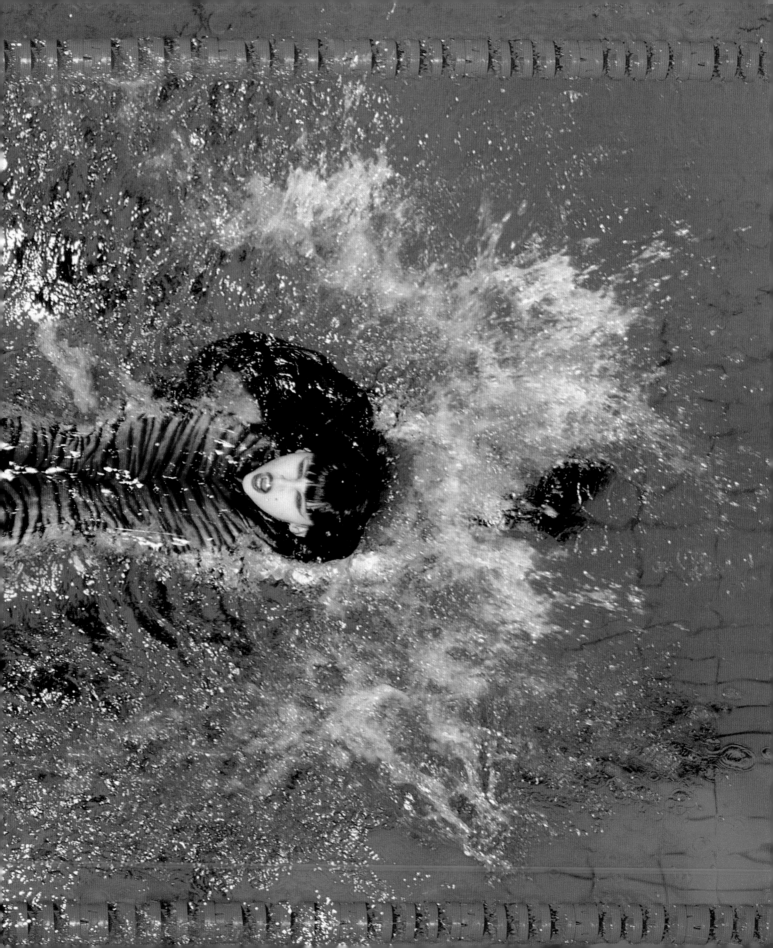

He's the highest paid lover in Beverly Hills.

He leaves women feeling more alive than they've ever felt before.

Except one.

American Gigolo

SCOTTIE

DERRICK

DREW

WAL

50

JASON

51

ELUSHA

52

TIM

DAV

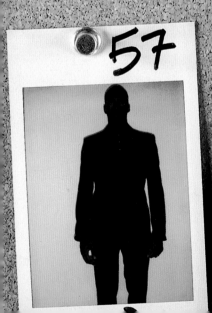

57

58

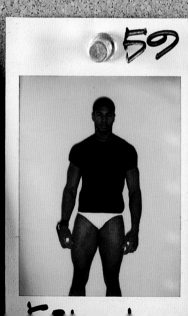

59

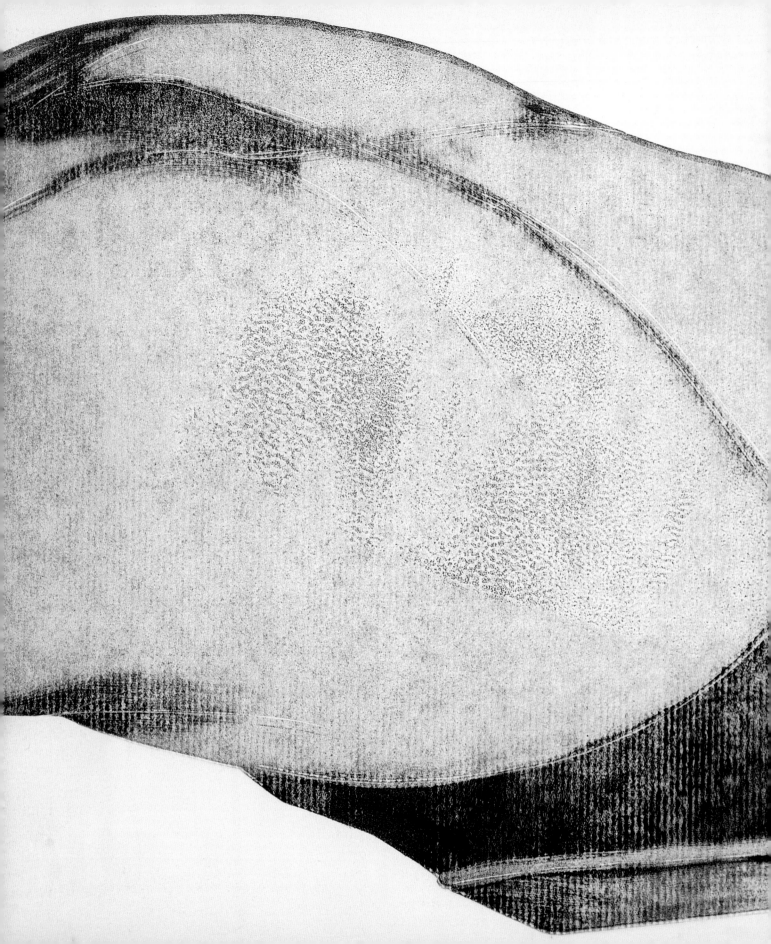

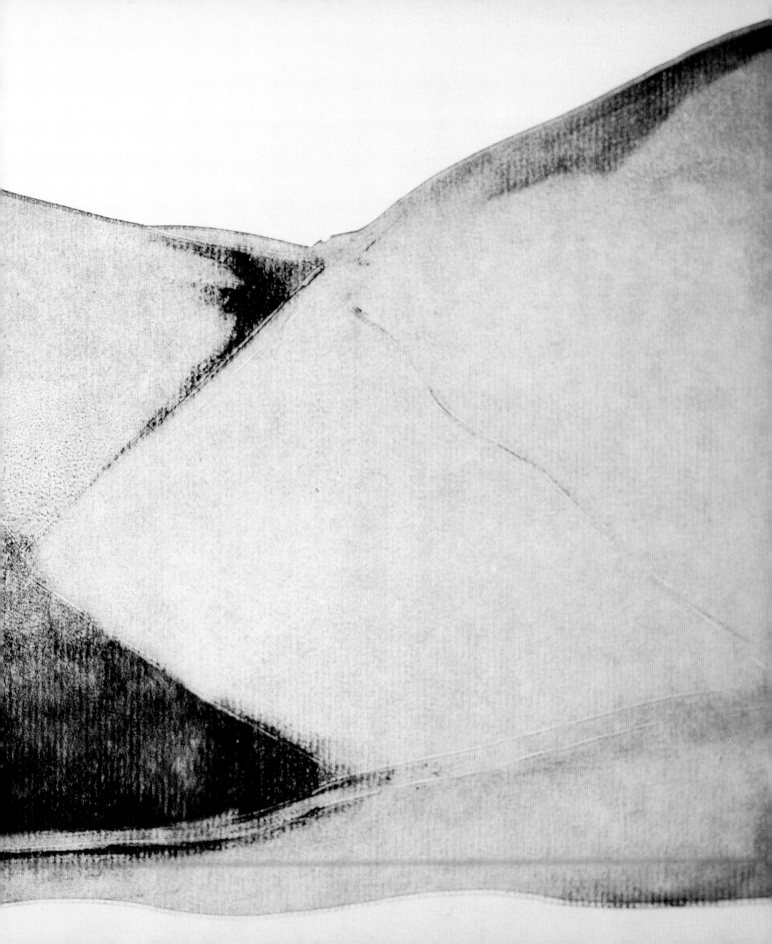

BERNADETTE CORPORATION
est. 1993
Photographed by Wolfgang Tillmans

Bernadette Corporation is a self-described "Monkey Clan" and "Corporation of riffraff" whose primary raison d'être is to knock fashion's block off. The cheeky pranksters behind the label are stylist Bernadette van Huy, designer Thuy Pham, promotional director/manager/fund-raiser/all-around adhesive force D'antek, producer/designer Seth Shapiro, and a constantly revolving satellite group of artists, deejays, photographers, and other creatively like-minded types. The core Corporation's combined fashion credentials include degrees in architecture, film, media studies, and cultural theo-

ry, as well as a cunning understanding of post-Cartesian cutting technique and a daring escape from a religious cult. The group first surfaced in 1993 when it began producing installations/parties/happenings in various nightclubs, parking garages, and storefronts throughout the greater downtown New York area. It wasn't long before BC discovered fashion to be a highly cooperative and opportune medium for its antics. The fashion shows they've presented have come across like a ride on New York's BDQ subway or a graduation pageant at an unaccredited beauty school. But underneath the junk heap of lowbrow popular culture that decorates the surface and serves as a stylistic playground for BC's ideas on such "problematic conditions" as mass production and socioeconomic politics lie some downright sophisticated notions of tailoring and construction. Champions of the disenfranchised, arbiters of bad taste, Bernadette Corporation doesn't merely hide out on the fringes of fashion throwing rocks and empty soda cans; it stands solidly behind fashion's back, poking, taunting, aping it at every turn, and ultimately begging it to swing around and take a punch.

BIKKEMBERGS, DIRK
b. 1962, Germany
Photographed by Roxanne Lowit

A graduate of Antwerp's Royal Academy of Arts and a former serviceman in the Royal Belgian Army, Dirk Bikkembergs has a way with footgear that comes through in his clothing like a sturdy steel-capped kick. He excels at thick slices of brightly colored knitwear, motorcycle leathers, and macho military imagery. He once created a series of jackets with laces and huge metal eyes—like a pair of combat boots transformed into a suit. This fortitude carries over into his women's line, which was born out of the men's line in 1993 and is aptly called Dirk Bikkembergs Homme—Pour la Femme.

BLAHNIK (cont.)
Photographed by (from left) Marcello Bertoni (Manolo Blahnik 1996 Florence Biennale installation) and Raymond Meier

< Blahniks are one of the greatest fashion vices of all time. The classic Manolo (the shoes are affectionately referred to on a first-name basis) has a toe box sharpened to fine point and a spindly, sculpted heel to match. To walk any distance greater than to the ladies' room and back in a pair of them requires several years' worth of childhood ballet lessons or the assistance of a walker (not walker as in crutch, but walker as in the arm of a handsome young man). Manolos can be the epitome of gentility or the height of eccentricity. Virginal champagne satin bridal slippers and tasteful

crocodile pumps stand alongside such vertiginous wonders as gladiator stilettos fitted with rosebud straps that creep up the leg like ivy on a trellis; tinkling sandals executed in dove gray ribbon and decked with miniature bells that snake around the big toe, heel, and ankle; or roughly hewn brown leather hiking shoes set high atop a Grand Teton of a stacked heel and a sliver of a lug sole. (The first real Manolos, which date back to the early '70s, were men's saddle shoes Blahnik designed for a shop in London called Zapata; in the same decade, he also invented the clear jelly

fisherman's sandal for Fiorucci.) Manolos are the kinds of shoes that make men whistle, women swoon, and hemlines go up. Perhaps the only group the dashing, silver-haired shoe designer has yet to win over is the orthopedic surgeons (something that has to do with the connection between four-inch spikes and back and foot problems). But surely even they can't deny the way a pair of Manolos can simultaneously lift a woman's spirit and her carriage, make her stand absolutely straight, shoulders back, chin up, as if she were walking on a cloud . . . or balancing a very full martini on her head.

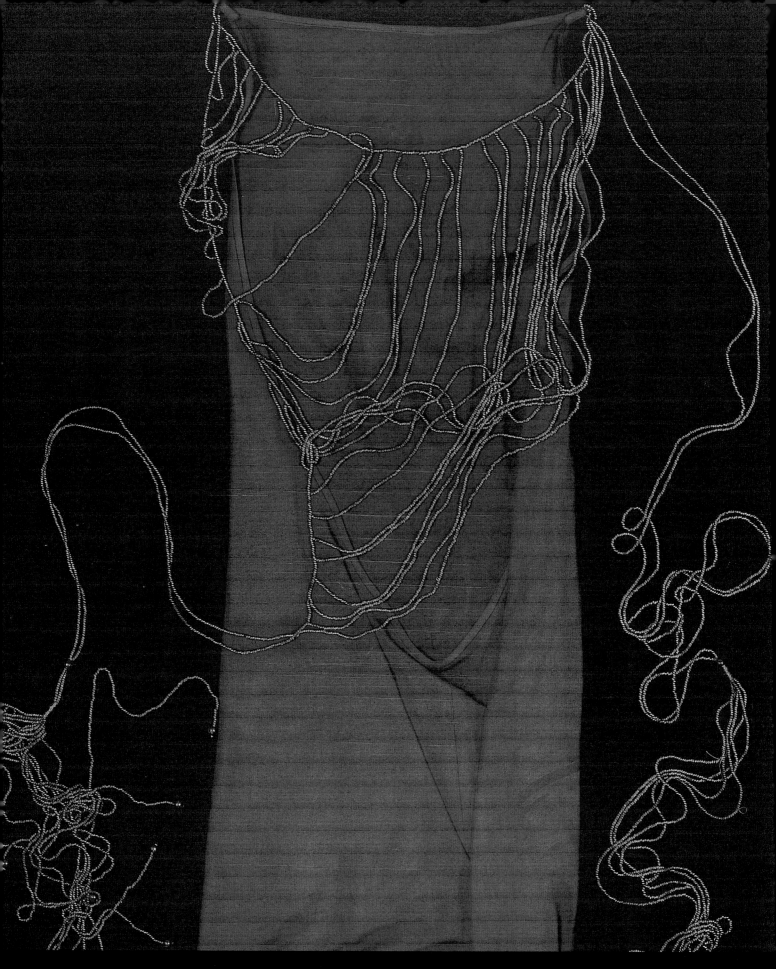

CHALAYAN, HUSSEIN
b. 1970, Cyprus
Photographed by Katerina Jebb

Hussein Chalayan once created an entire collection from weather patterns. "I go through a series of processes," he says. "I have a thought. I create a feeling around the thought. The thought branches out into different ideas. Eventually the ideas become symbols and the symbols become prints. It takes its own course." Chalayan graduated from St. Martins College of Art in 1993 and presented his first solo collection in the spring of the following year. Equal parts philosopher, tailor, and sorcerer, Chalayan rejects the obvious reference. His insistence on showing fashion something

deeper than the new black or higher than the new length has manifest itself in such collections as Temporary Interference ("the absurdity demonstrated by jumping off bridge heights in the hope of being saved by an exterior force"); Along False Equator ("a repetitive pattern of sensation felt in the womb and sustained in our daily lives through our experience of rhythm, speed, and sound"); and Scent of Tempests ("by looking at the elemental changes as a life force, the weather acquires a Godly connotation with undertones of worship and ritual"). Cryptic as it may sound, the transla-

tion is always more suggestive than literal: aerodynamic jackets that twinkle with a spray of red destination lights; glow-in-the-dark pantsuits in light-sensitive paper; dresses adorned with beaded overlays to give them the aura of sacred objects. Chalayan's fantastic flights are grounded in his belief that clothing must break the bounds of convention within the realm of the wearable. Chalayan has an innate understanding of fashion's potential to fill the space between fantasy and reality, between clothing as a means to cover the body and clothing as a way to send the spirit soaring

naive, Cianciolo's work often lacks the conventional markers that identify a garment or that indicate just how it is meant to be put on. Free-form knitting, deconstructed denim, uneven hand-dying and stitching, industrial fabrics… "Clothing to me is a personal interest and a medium," she says. Cianciolo attended Rhode Island School of Design and Parsons in New York and Paris; she has worked for such disparate fashion companies as Badgley Mischka, X-Girl, and Geoffrey Beene. When she presented her first collection in 1995, which she describes as "asymmetric and American street-influenced," she had also been working as a freelance fashion illustrator for two years. In Cianciolo's fall 1997 collection, shown in a rattletrap space that once housed a retail concern called Glamour Furniture, models pulled clothing from tiny handbags and dressed themselves before the audience or peeled off odd layers as they made their way down the makeshift runway. "I began from random and abstract shapes formed by hand stitching and some under- and over-sized pieces," she says. "It seems to me that anything becomes recognizable as clothing if it is worn."

COLONNA (cont.)
Photographed by Frédérique du Moulin

< up as an accessories designer. He started his own label in 1985, presenting his first collections as catalogs and staging his first show in 1990. Exposed seams and a gritty, biker attitude established him as a rebel with deconstructionist tendencies. "People thought that I was violent, a destroyer," he said. Instead, Colonna, who cites Coco Chanel as a model, has tried to create an authentic glamour that he and the women he loves can relate to. "Chic is not just a bourgeois thing; it has nothing to do with money," he has said. "Making choices for the way you live, to me that is luxury."

DELL'ACQUA, ALESSANDRO
b. 1963, Italy
Photographed by Carter Smith

Alessandro Dell'Acqua is one young designer working to change Milan's reputation from a manufacturing mecca to a hotbed of fashion. His collections don't stand on tailored sensibility, they smoulder with ultrafine knits, lace, and jersey. For twelve years, Dell'Acqua worked for Italian powerhouses: Genny, Gilmar—companies that offer solid commercial grounding but don't necessarily nourish the imagination. But when Dell'Acqua presented his first collection in 1996, he did so with a passion befitting his Neopolitan heritage. "Not much romanticism," he said. "Lots of sensuality instead."

arrive at something and find that other people have been waiting for it, too." A fiercely independent spirit, Demeulemeester has stayed on a steady course since she founded her company with her husband and partner, Patrick Robyn, in 1985. Her first collection consisted of two small racks of clothes, which she presented in 1987 in a group show in London with five other graduates from Antwerp's Royal College of Arts. The fact that it was well received gave her the courage to go on. "I did everything my own way. Step by step," Demeulemeester says, "I didn't let anyone hurry me. It

sounds very easy but it involved a lot of hard work." Ann Demeulemeester is at once a problem creator and a problem solver, a perfectionist who finds inspiration through rigorous self-interrogation ("Designing for me is looking inside myself," she says). She will relentlessly pursue an idea from a hundred different angles (using her own body as a dress form), until she makes it work. When she was designing her spring 1995 collection, for example, she became fixed on the concept of cutting movement and balance into her clothing. The picture in her mind was of a trouser that slid away >

As Italian fashion slouched its way into the '90s, Domenico Dolce and Stefano Gabbana, the duo behind Dolce & Gabbana, emerged to inject a shot of va-va-voom. If the softly tailored jacket had come to stand for Italian fashion, Dolce & Gabbana proposed instead the corset. Drawing on the films of Roberto Rossellini and Luchino Visconti, images of Anna Magnani, Sophia Loren, and Isabella Rossellini (who would appear in their ad campaigns), and their own Italian heritage, Dolce & Gabbana harnessed the power of the female body. Dolce, a "de facto Sicilian," is from Palermo;

FORD, TOM
b. 1962, Texas
Photographed by Inez van Lamsweerde & Vinoodh Matadin

One of the first big decisions Tom Ford made as the newly appointed creative director for Gucci was to give the company's signature crossed Gs a rest. The Gs were old, tired, overexposed; Ford preferred to play up discreet variations on the snaffle bit instead. But Gs or no Gs, there was no need to spell it out: the power label was back (and anyway, a few seasons later the Gs would be back for another round, too). Ford, who says he does some of his best research checking out the international club scene and insists that "retro" is not a dirty word, revamped the Gucci image by drawing heavily

upon the glamour days of the label's jet-set past. To this he added a splash of swinging London, images of Halston and Yves Saint Laurent, souvenirs from the swanky Studio 54 '70s (a time when the beige leather interior of a Cadillac really *meant* something), the brazen chic of Cleopatra Jones, a certain James Bond *suaveté*, and filtered it all through the critical sieve of his own '90s sensibility ("Is it modern?" is Ford's constant litmus test). It was just the right cocktail (shaken, not stirred) of conspicuous luxury and sexual promiscuity that a decidedly post-Gucci generation—reared on

Grunge, used Levis, and fleeting images of the way mom and dad used to dress—was craving. Tom Ford was born in Texas and raised in Santa Fe. At seventeen, he skipped out to the big city to attend New York University but dropped out as a sophomore to become an actor. Several ads for McDonald's, Old Spice, and Prell shampoo later, he enrolled himself in the interior design program at Parsons in Los Angeles and then transferred to the school's Paris campus. It was there that he realized some-thing he might have figured out the day he was twelve years old and begged his mom for a pair of

FORD (cont.)
Photographed by Mario Testino

< white Gucci loafers—what he really wanted to be was a fashion designer. Ford earned a design internship at Chloé, moved back to New York to work for Cathy Hardwick in 1986, and two years later was hired by Marc Jacobs at Perry Ellis. Still, Ford was a less-than-proven quantity when he was called upon by Dawn Mello to develop Gucci's first full women's ready-to-wear line in 1990, a time when the only interesting Gucci stories were about family feuds and impending financial disaster. And then, when the investment bank Investcorp, which had taken a 50 percent stake in

the Gucci business in 1988, instituted a scale-back, Ford found himself designing almost everything under the Gucci label. (Perhaps the first clue that something exciting was afoot at Gucci came in 1993, when Ford transformed the tried-and-true Gucci snaffle loafer into a chunky suede clog. A few seasons later it came slinking out on a sleek stiletto heel.) After Mello left in 1994, Ford was promoted to creative director, responsible for the design of eleven product categories, as well as visual display and advertising. Detail-obsessed and focused to a fault, Ford sent Gucci into turnaround mode; he even went so far as to tweak the green Gucci shopping bag to a shade of almost-black. Ford's big secret, of course, is that Gucci is a commercially viable product—it's just a commercially viable product sexed up to the nth degree of desirability. After years of general fashion denial, Ford is pushing the right buttons, bringing back the days when people lusted for fashion—when people lusted for Gucci. The question remains, however, will we all wake up one morning to a massive Gucci hangover and a lot of buyer's remorse? Perhaps, but not anytime in this century.

GALLIANO, JOHN
b. 1960, Gibraltar
Photographed by Jean-Paul Goude

John Galliano's descent on the fashion world was like the crash of a gilded chandelier: no one really saw him coming, and afterward they couldn't believe what had hit them. Fashion in the sober early '90s had been looking for reality, a sensible leg on which to stand—Galliano gave them pure fly-by-the-seat-of-your-pants fantasy. Words such as pretty, feminine, and magical were uttered for the first time in a very long time and with real conviction. Stylistically speaking, Galliano is often referred to as a magpie, a designer who pinches a Poiret silhouette here, plucks a Dior line there,

picks up a Navajo blanket somewhere else entirely, and then, with a clever turn of seam, makes them his own. He is a deft and obsessive fashion historian who reconstructs the past with a heady dose of poetic license. His clothes can be impossibly complex: wickedly cut jackets with lapels that vanish into the shoulderline, deceptive slipdresses with labyrinth seaming that take a stunning twist into the shape of an orchid or a swirl of ribbon. To be fair, Galliano didn't drop out of the sky. The son of a plumber, he graduated from St. Martins in 1984. His graduation collection, Les

Incroyables, caught initial attention, but financial stability proved elusive for this most eccentric of the British Eccentrics; backers came courting and went. Some ten years later he finally got an honest proposal and the wherewithal to establish John Galliano S.A.R.L. In the fall of 1994, Galliano produced the collection that knocked the fashion world off its minimalist axis. Three seasons later he was tapped to take over the house of Givenchy. He didn't hold the post long: in January 1997 he presented his first couture collection as the designer of Dior. The fashion world is still reeling.

GALLIANO (cont.)
Photographed by Mario Testino, Laurent Van Der Stockt (b/w),
Dan and Corina Lecca (runway), and Roxanne Lowit (top row, second from right)

GARAVANI, VALENTINO
b. 1932, Italy
Photograph courtesy of Valentino

For more than thirty-five years, the House of Valentino has stood as a sort of temple to the pretty, the feminine, the enchanting. Frilly, frothy dresses in floral chiffon, sometimes beaded or embroidered with the most delicate of hands, and neat day suits with fitted jackets that gently emphasize the waist, and shortish skirts to show the legs to advantage, have always had a place in Valentino's collections—and in his heart. Valentino never tires of beautiful things—and beautiful women (Babe Paley, Jackie Onassis, and Sharon Stone have all worn his clothes). It is impossible to

imagine him even entertaining the thought of dabbling in the distasteful, not even on a lark. Valentino (who was named after the silent film star) studied fashion at the Accademia dell'Arte in Milan and the Chambre Syndicale de la Couture in Paris. He worked as an assistant to the Greek designer Jean Dessès and then to Guy Laroche, and in 1960 he opened his own fashion house in Rome. In 1968, he showed a breathtaking all-white collection at the Pitti Palace in Florence that secured him a notice in fashion history. But Valentino's signature shade is red, a color that first struck him when he was a student visiting Barcelona. Valentino's exhibition at the Florence Biennale, nearly thirty years after the white show, was a display of red gowns that both complimented and flirted shamelessly with Michelangelo's statue of David across the room. What makes Valentino more than a pure classicist, and more than a society lady's designer, is the fact that he has never sealed himself off from the times. He knows how to tip the balance with a soupçon of sex. As he once told *W* magazine, "The essence of Valentino style is femininity... femininity and seduction."

GAULTIER, JEAN-PAUL
b. 1952, France
Photographed by (from left) Corina Lecca and Inez van Lamsweerde & Vinoodh Matadin

Jean-Paul Gaultier is the ringleader of a traveling circus. He has taken fashion on carousel rides through the twentieth century from bustles to bra tops, on rollicking gallops through Mongolia, Tibet, China, Morocco, and Harlem, and on a whirlwind trip around the world in 168 outfits. His entourage includes men and women mapped in elaborate head-to-toe tattoos and shot full of body piercings; half-man–half-woman creatures (the result, no doubt, of a gender-bending collision); and an ever-changing cast of Rabbis, sorceresses, gigolos, Vikings, Pharaohs, cancan girls, cow-

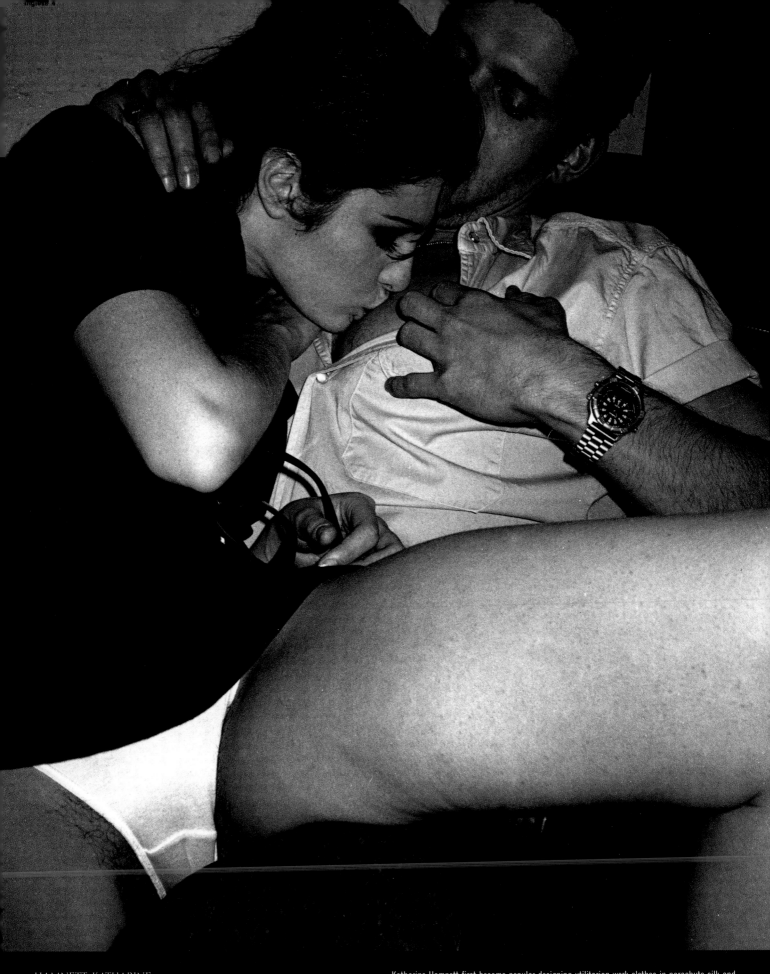

HAMNETT, KATHARINE
b. 1948, England
Photographed Terry Richardson

Katharine Hamnett first became popular designing utilitarian work clothes in parachute silk and cotton drill, but her legend turned on a 1983 line of white T-shirts emblazoned with bold, block-lettered slogans such as WORLDWIDE NUCLEAR BAN NOW and HEROIN-FREE ZONE. In the '90s, Hamnett is more about action than words: instrumental in the Pesticides Trust Sustainable Cotton Program, she runs an environmentally correct company. But as her punchy denim line and the accompanying ad campaigns testify, underneath all that political correctness still lurks a provocateur

JACOBS, MARC
b. 1963, New York
Photographed by Larry Fink (b/w) and Dan Lecca (runway)

Marc Jacobs would be the first to tell you that there is nothing extraordinary about the clothing he designs. It's not classic; it's not fashiony; it doesn't aspire to the cutting edge. It just sort of *is*. But Marc Jacobs would be lying. First of all, his taste level won't allow him to make just any old clothes. He has an expensive habit for fabrics such as double-faced cashmere, cut perversely on the bias. Anything he touches—from ribbed tanks to slip dresses that look as if they were spun from gold—rarely comes up short of perfection. What does ring true, however, is Jacobs's self-effacing atti-

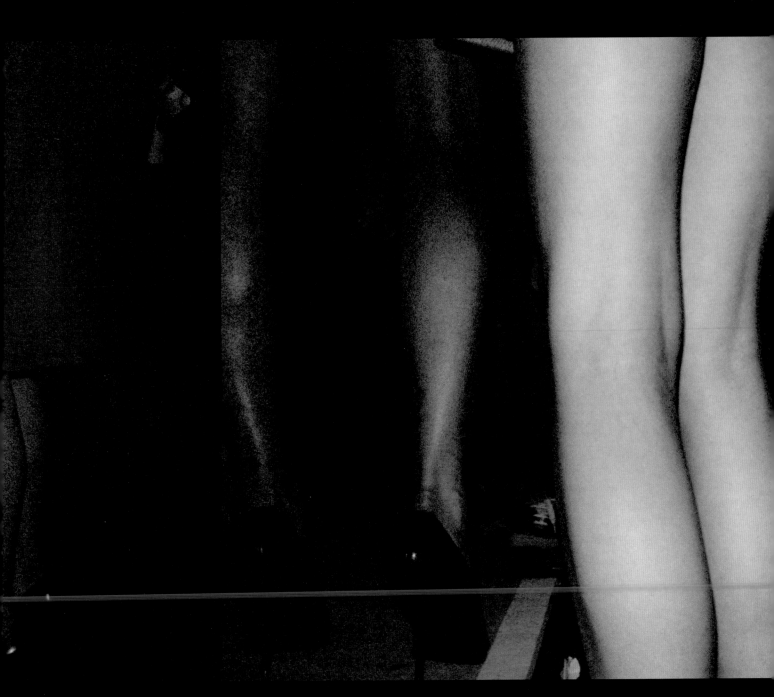

a brief but high-profile appearance in 1986 that ended in 1988 when a fire destroyed his spring collection; the following year Jacobs was hired by Perry Ellis as vice president of women's wear. His Perry Ellis collections were refined and rooted in classics but rollicked with a freewheeling spirit played out in vibrant colors and witty trompe l'oeil effects. But in 1992, when he put Grunge on the runway, it was widely assumed that he had taken one liberty too many. Even as Jacobs was lauded by the CFDA as designer of the year he also lost his job. In 1994 he came back with a new collec- tion under his own name, a show of skewed sophistication inspired by New York in the '70s. In 1996 he joined Louis Vuitton as artistic director where he would develop the company's first ready-to- wear line. To this day, Jacobs likes to think of Grunge as the best collection he ever did, a feeling inspired by the freedom to mix things up, to not look so perfect, to wear your shirt untucked even if that shirt costs upwards of three hundred dollars. "It's still an attitude that influences the way people dress today," Jacobs told *W* magazine. In spirit, he's been designing that very collection ever since.

JOHNSON, BETSEY
b. 1942, Connecticut
Photographed by Robert Mapplethorpe

When Betsey Johnson was young, she wanted to be a cheerleader and a cake decorator. Instead, she became a designer applying her exuberance to Paraphernalia in the '60s and to Alley Cat in the '70s. In 1978, she established her own label, a dream-come-true because it gave her total creative control. Control, however, is not a word that fits Betsey's bill. Out of control? Maybe. Wacky? Yes. Fun? Definitely. Give me a tube top! Give me a catsuit! Give me a dragon brocade coat! Betsey is fashion's cheerleader; she still comes out at the end of her shows to perform a cartwheel and a split.

KARAN, DONNA
b. 1948, New York
Photographed by Larry Fink

Donna Karan talks about herself a lot—but this is what makes her a good designer. Karan takes fashion personally; she is her own inspiration, her own muse, her own reality-check. She studied fashion at Parsons but left in her second year to work for Anne Klein, where she rose to design director in 1974. She launched Donna Karan New York in 1985 with the idea of creating a set of clothes for her and a few of her friends. But as more and more women caught on to her we're-all-in-the-same-boat-here mentality, Karan discovered she had more "friends" than she ever imagined.

hausted every design possibility in black, and that it was drained of its prior strength from overuse. (Florals were to appear the next season in Flowering Clothes.) Then there was Kawakubo's spring 1997 collection, Body Becomes Dress, Dress Becomes Body. "I don't remember when or how I got the inspiration," she told Japanese *Marie Claire* of her series of body-defining Lycra dresses outfitted with body-redefining, down-filled bulges (some of which were stuffed with enough feathers to fill an entire duvet). "It was as if anesthesia suddenly wore off or I had recovered from amnesia." In the wake of the controversy and confusion stirred up by the collection in all of its lumpy alternativeness, Comme des Garçons released an all-points bulletin explaining not how the humps were supposed to be positioned (much less sold) but why, in some much greater sense, they had appeared there in the first place. "Not what has been seen before. Not what has been repeated. Instead, new discoveries that look towards the future, that are liberated and lively. This is Comme des Garçons' approach to creating clothes. The spring/summer collection has arrived."

KERRIGAN, DARYL
b. 1965, Ireland
Photographed by Inez van Lamsweerde & Vinoodh Matadin

New York designer Daryl Kerrigan walks the walk of a cool street-savvy girl. Her groovy vibe, a mix of punk, country-western, and ambient drum, plays to a young urban sensibility in the form of draw-string and hipster pants, tube tops and camisoles, slashed sweaters and simple dresses sliced through with glimpses of sheerness, and is quickly setting the pace for downtown fashion at the end of the '90s. "I grew up wanting to dress a certain way and getting flak for it," Kerrigan told *Elle* magazine. "I just hate to see people getting laughed at for expressing themselves through their

part on the inside, as an early design influence. His high-end Collection line, one of the few that Klein has not licensed out, epitomizes this casual elegance: streamlined and functional, luxurious on the sly. But there is little question that Klein's pared-down aesthetic also fits nicely with his taste for commercial success. It's assimilate. Distill. Sell. Klein's marketing acumen kicks into overdrive at the lower end of his range. His controversial ads push the limits of propriety, even as the products they push on the national subconscious are, beneath their gloss of sex and, well, more

sex, fundamentally safe. Brooke Shields in blue jeans; Marky Mark in white cotton briefs; spots featuring body-pierced, tattooed "real people" who share a fragrance from a twist-top bottle; or teenagers shot in a '70s basement rec room scenario, creepily interrogated by an unseen man whose voice insinuates rumpled-trenchcoat-with-nothing-underneath (another message to buy CK jeans). When Klein was invited to show at AIDS Project Los Angeles, his finale was a parade of nubile young models scantily dressed in white cotton underwear. But not just any white cotton underwear. Calvins.

KORS, MICHAEL
b. 1959, New York
Photographed by David Lasnett

Michael Kors has ventured from the country club scene to the night club scene, but the common thread running through his fifteen-year body of work has always been his taste for minimalism and his understanding of the American dynamic. Kors studied at Fashion Institute of Technology and worked as a sales assistant for Lothar's. He moved up to designer and display director before launching his signature label in 1981. In the tradition of Halston, Kors's combination of low-key luxe and T-shirt simplicity give the term "American sportswear" not only a nice ring, but an edge.

LACROIX, CHRISTIAN
b. 1951, France
Photographed by Irving Penn

When Christian Lacroix made his haute couture debut in 1987, he was the first designer to open a new house in Paris since Yves Saint Laurent more than twenty-five years earlier. It has been suggested that Lacroix happened to have been in the right place at a time when new money and opulence were at an all-time high, but the fact of the matter is nobody can ruche, ruffle, flounce, lace, bead, embroider, and re-embroider the way Lacroix can—and this all on a single evening dress. Lacroix brings to fashion both a fearless eccentricity and a willingness to lay the fantasy on thick. >

LACROIX (cont.)
Photographed by Roxanne Lowit

< *Do you believe that it was fate that made you a designer?* I don't hide my strong belief in divinatory arts, mediums, numerology, and especially astrology. To be born under the sign of Taurus in a family of bullfighting aficionados and in a land where we breed bulls (the Camargue), plus the sign of Leo in my ascendant in the city of Arles for which the lion is a symbol—all of this seems predestined and very symptomatic of my stubbornness, my tenacity, my sensual attachment to things from the earth as much as the pride, taste for the flamboyant, and a certain authority which are all quite

necessary ingredients to work in the fashion field. *What is the most complicated piece of clothing you've ever created?* Each garment always seems complicated to me in the sense that all of them must be amazing as well as wearable. The search for invisible understructures that must create a silhouette (shoulder pads, corsets, underskirts) especially in couture, is also fascinating, just like superimposing different techniques of craftwork on a single garment (weaving, painting, embroidery): lace patchwork, watercolored and embroidered wedding gowns, metallic forms directly shaped to the body, fabrics specially weaved to the client's form, countless meters of chiffon that become invisible once made into a sheath dress, unlikely fabrics worked into unnatural architectures with the help of horse hair, wire, and other atelier secrets. *Have you ever made anything simple?* Maybe a T-shirt, a seamless knotted bra, or lace panties? *What has been your greatest moment in fashion?* The cheers of my friends from the South at my first show, just like at a bullfight; the Molière award for best costumes in Phèdre (1996); tears in the eyes of clients at the end of a show.

LAGERFELD, KARL
b. 1938, Germany
Photographed by Karl Lagerfeld

Karl Lagerfeld is one of the most parodied figures in fashion (the fan, the sunglasses, the powdered hair, the accent as thick and as impenetrably fuzzy as alpaca). He is also, without a doubt, the most prolific and the most powerful. When a malingering fashion house cries out for a Karl Lagerfeld, what it means is a fashion Terminator who can come in with an innate understanding of the power of a label and a rat-a-tat-tat of new ideas and blow everyone away. Several houses have been so lucky as to get Lagerfeld in their camp. There have been years when Lagerfeld has designed as

three-button jackets, tank and T-shirts, and slip dresses. ("My collections have always included pants, jackets, dresses," he has said, providing no further description.) These archetypal pieces, relentlessly urban, often directly inspired by the street and tailored to the realities of life at the end of the twentieth century, are the components of the modern uniform; their integrity—and no small amount of cachet—derives from their essential understatedness and their apparent simplicity. Helmut Lang came to fashion via the Viennese art world. He established his design studio in 1977 in Vienna and opened a made-to-measure shop in 1979. He held his first ready-to-wear presentation—a collection for women—in Paris in 1986; he showed a menswear line in Paris the following year. Lang has taught a masterclass in fashion at the University of Applied Arts in Vienna since 1993. These are the official facts on file. Lang remains one of the most enigmatic names on the fashion roster. For him to reveal much more than absolutely necessary would be superfluous and just plain out of character. From the perspective of the '80s, Lang's early collections caught fash- >

LANG (cont.)
Photographed by (from left) Nan Goldin and Jürgen Teller

< ion completely off-guard. They were expecting to see *something*, but he showed them practically *nothing*. His models marched through the crowd at ground level, stone-faced and serious. There was no runway, no theatrics, and like modern art seen for the first time, what was immediately striking about his clothes was a sense of absence. But like the apparently blank canvas that upon closer inspection reveals thousands of tiny brush strokes, Lang's minimalism is deceptive; there is always something more to his clothes if you know to look for it. A tank dress, for example, might be

next thing Julien knew, *poof!*, he was whisked off to Paris to become the knitwear designer for Chanel ready-to-wear, Chanel Couture, and Karl Lagerfeld. On high, Julien returned to London and in the spring of 1997 he presented his own collection, entitled Mermaids, an homage to the "Mermaid Lady of the Blue Grotto" whom Julien believes he saw when he was ten years old on a summer visit to Capri with his family. "I wanted to create a fairy-tale evening," Julien says. "To send a message that people would always keep in their hearts." There was a dress that had been knitted from horse hair

and another so finely wrought it was almost completely transparent and trimmed at the hem with seventeenth-century embroidery that Julien had pulled from a chair he had stumbled upon in the street on his travels to Paris. Julien's amazingly intricate dresses, produced in only four-of-a-kind, are spun from a high-tech twist of viscose/silk/cashmere/polyamide yarn using a painstaking combination of new-fangled machinery and old-world artisanship. "They are as light as a feather," exclaims Julien. "No! Light as a cloud!" And as magical and ethereal as the vision that inspired them

MARGIELA, MARTIN
b. 1957, Belgium
Photographed by Inez van Lamsweerde & Vinoodh Matadin

Martin Margiela graduated from Antwerp's Royal Academy of Arts in 1979. After a brief stint as the assistant to Jean-Paul Gaultier, Margiela opened his own design house in Paris in 1988. He presented his first Paris collection the following year. In 1997, he was hired to oversee the collections at the house of Hermès. Margiela is often thought of as *the deconstructionist*, the designer who ripped open fashion in the '90s at its seams. Recycled clothing, unraveling hems, garment parts as opposed to whole pieces (sleeves and collars detached from their torsos), and blank white labels

Theirry Mugler lives in a '50s Hollywood sci-fi fashion thriller with an N.C.-17 rating. The starring cast of Muglerettes can appear dressed for the role of an elegant insect, an exquisite android (part model, part motorcycle), or an aerodynamic amazon woman from Mars. Mugler was raised on a steady diet of "horror movies, Italian cinema, and Hollywood musicals." At fourteen, he joined the Opera du Rhin dance company and later studied at the Strasbourg School for the Decorative Arts. At twenty, Mugler moved to Paris, where his personal style found an audience on the terrace of Café de

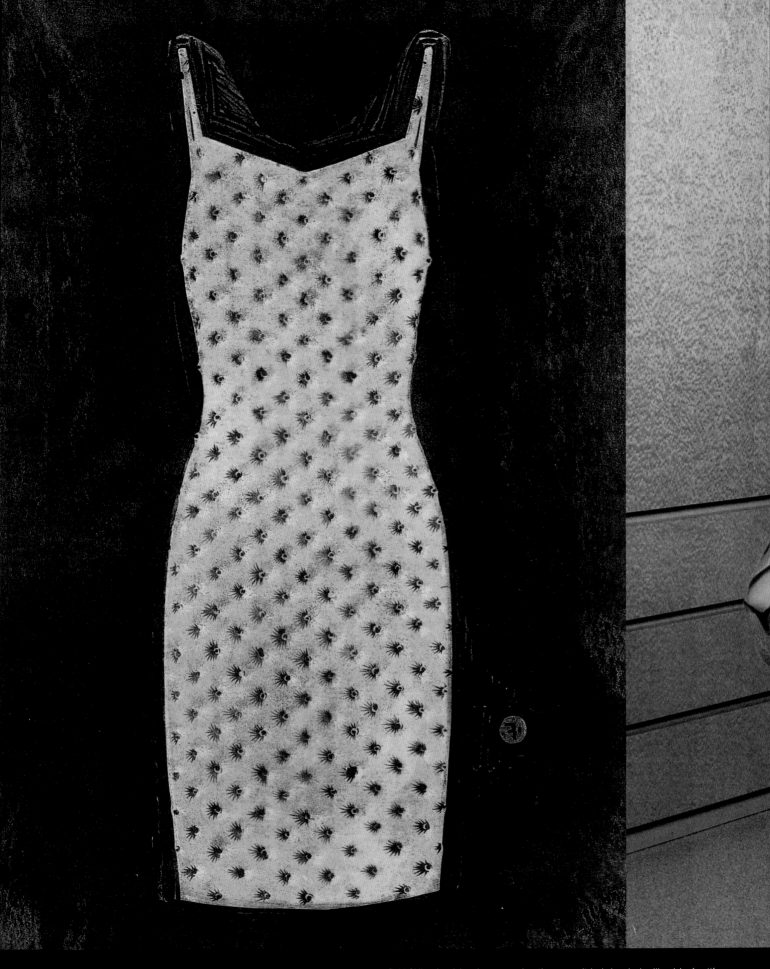

OLDHAM, TODD
b. 1961, Texas
Illustrated by François Berthoud; photographed by Inez van Lamsweerde & Vinoodh Matadin

Todd Oldham's rainbow has more colors than yours. It includes shades like glob-of-antifreeze-baking-in-the-sun-green, cheap-motel-bedspread-pink, and rec-room-paneling brown. Once Todd showed a whopping 1,755 colors in the range—all at once—in a single dress done up like mosaic tile. It was quite a spectacle. Some people have probably wondered if Todd isn't perhaps color blind the way he mixes up no-no combinations of pink-and-orange or purple-and-green, not to mention plaids with plaids with stripes, or animal prints with animal prints. But the truth is he gets a thrill

from seeing the way the colors, patterns, and textures interact. For Todd, designing a collection must be like throwing a huge party where none of the invitees have ever met before. By some stroke of luck—or simply because the guests are all friends of Todd's—the conversation always sparkles brilliantly. Todd never had a traditional fashion education, unless you count working in the alterations department at Ralph Lauren in Dallas when he was nineteen. There is a loving-hands, arts-and-crafts feeling to everything he touches. (His MTV *House of Style* segments promoted do-it-

yourself fashion such as cutting Dad's old shirt into a halter top.) À la mode bricolage, his collections are a kaleidoscopic collage of embroidery, beading, crochet, fringe, photoprints, watercolors, and paint-by-numbers masterpieces. Taking stock of the tag sales and trailer parks across America, Todd has created suits from trompe l'oeil cork and long slinky dresses from Grandma's macramé throw. His clothes are always done with humor and can be sexy as all get out—bad taste served up with a big smile. "I don't make clothes that are funny," he has said, "I make clothes that are fun."

OZBEK, RIFAT
b. 1953, Istanbul
Photographed by Patrick Demarchelier

Rifat Ozbek came to England from Turkey in 1970, fully intending to become an architect but discovered, in the course of his studies at Liverpool University, that engineering didn't inspire him as much as decorating. After three years Ozbek moved to London and enrolled in the fashion program at St. Martins; he created his first collection in 1984. Dubbed the Sultan of Style, Ozbek took fashion on a magic carpet ride to Tibet, Senegal, and his native Istanbul. His vibrant, multicultural aesthetic plays out in tribal markings, plumes of feathers, and breastplates created from "bones."

PRADA, MIUCCIA
b. c. 1950, Italy
Photographed by (from left) Glen Luchford and Mario Sorrenti

A Label Is Born. One of the biggest stories of the '90s is the runaway tale of the Italian leather goods company that stole the international fashion spotlight. It stars a black nylon backpack and one Miuccia Prada, a woman who is, by her own admission, the unlikeliest of fashion heroines. Miuccia Prada holds a Ph.D in political science and was an upstanding and active member of the communist party in the '70s. In contrast to the feminist wardrobe of jeans and T-shirts, Prada wore antique dresses and occasional designer ensembles, but fashion was something she resisted. In

PRADA (cont.)
Photographed by Bill Cunningham

SAINT LAURENT, YVES
b. 1936, Algeria
Left, courtesy of Yves Saint Laurent; right, photographed by Mario Testino

In 1957, Yves Saint Laurent became the chief designer of Christian Dior at the age of twenty-one. His three-year tenure ended when he designed a collection that featured crocodile motorcycle jackets. Too hip for his own good—or Dior's own good, at least. But this Left Bank look was the beginning of a fashion revolution. Saint Laurent was to become the very first designer whose initials—YSL—carried meaning. It has been several seasons since the designer has turned that inevitable corner from fashion innovator to fashion source of inspiration. His prolific thirty-five-year career

has been edited down to a singular definition of what-it-means-to-be-chic and a handful of telling examples: the shiny black patent mini-trench worn by housewife-with-a-secret-life Catherine Deneuve in Luis Bunuel's film *Belle de Jour*; the sleekly tailored pantsuit captured in all its aggressive androgyny by photographer Helmut Newton in 1975; the Pagoda jacket once worn by Diana Vreeland; the luxe full-skirted peasant looks; and the YSL tuxedo, dubbed Le Smoking, the smoldering sophistication of which has yet to be paralleled and probably never will be. Petits homages to

Saint Laurent's collections from les années '70s have appeared in late '90s collections by designers such as Marc Jacobs, Tom Ford, Miuccia Prada, and Helmut Lang. Established Paris houses are all looking for a young visionary—John Galliano? Alexander McQueen?—who can make the same waves and the same magic. At the end of the millennium, Saint Laurent's genius resides more in fashion's nostalgia for a glamorous past than it does in the actual present, but if presence can be measured in influence then the spirit of Saint Laurent is as alive today as it was twenty years ago.

not how Sander's clothes *feel*; her pragmatism belies a deep sensuality. "I design clothes that have a very personal and quiet feeling of ease and self-confidence for women and men who wish to feel attractive and modern," Sander says, point blank. Sander graduated from Dusseldorf's Krefeld School of Textiles in 1943. She entered fashion as a journalist. In 1968, she began working as a freelance designer: "I presented my first collection in 1973," Sander says. "Since that time my point of view has not changed. I have always believed in using the finest materials, very innovative

design, the highest standards of quality, and I have avoided excessive decoration." Sander's clothes have been called classic, a term she loathes because it implies an unwillingness to confront the present. She has also been referred to as a minimalist, but this word, with its suggestion of absence, of stripping away, doesn't suit either. "I have a strong vision for opulence which lies in clean, refined, and sophisticated design with an ultra-high standard," she says. "Fashion is about movement and creating a vision in a modern way reflecting the time in which we live and hopefully inspiring it."

SANDER (cont.)
Photographed by Nick Knight

Marquée Club at night and comb the flea markets in the early morning hours. Back home in Paris, she would tuck a transistor radio under her pillow at night and tune back into London. "When I started, my biggest influences came from the late '60s and early '70s rock-music scene," she says. "The Velvet Underground, the Stones, people like Nico, Edie Sedgwick, Lou Reed, Brian Jones." Sitbon graduated from Studio Berçot in Paris in 1974. After an extended journey to Asia, South America, and the United States, and several years as a freelance stylist and designer, Sitbon showed her first collection in 1985. "The theme was urban rock juxtaposed with the dream universe of Alice in Wonderland." For more than fifteen years, Sitbon's collaborator has been Marc Ascoli, the man largely responsible for the designer catalog craze. It was Ascoli, Sitbon says, who encouraged her to follow her own instincts. Indeed, Sitbon's collections can come across like a journey through the books she's read, the movies she's seen, music she's been listening to, places she's been. "It's a story which evolves," she says. "I have a clear idea when I start, but I don't know exactly where it's going to take me."

be conservative fashion creatures who take occasional flights to the land of eccentricity. "If you went on a jumbo jet and the pilot was dressed as a beach boy would you trust him to fly the plane?" Smith asks. "People shouldn't dress out of character, just dress to show their personality." Smith's own personality has come through in his signature photoprints (oranges, florals, chopped logs), quirky accessories such as cuff links made from typewriter keys, a green dinosaur raincoat (that he occasionally—and somewhat regrettably—still sees around), and most of all in his stores. At the end of the '90s, Smith has nearly two hundred shops worldwide, many of them done up to look like a gentleman's closet with oak floors and mahogany shelves and stocked with neat suits, antique metal toys, fish-shaped lamps, and vintage issues of *Playboy*—all things that fit into Smith's concept of "things for boys!" "It's so boring, I know, to be so enthusiastic all the time, but I just can't help it," he says in the catalog to *True Brit*, an exhibition celebrating his twenty-fifth year as a designer. "If I see something strange, or funny, or something I've not seen before, I want it."

them away in her "Genius files" for future reference. She has had her share of great fashion moments, too: growing up in Deerborn Heights, she was the girl in the class picture wearing the frilly lavender party dress; she made a lot of her own clothes—stitching up a wardrobe of dresses for herself and using the extra fabric and Elmer's glue to make matching shoes; and in ninth grade she was voted Best Dressed. Sui went to Parsons School of Design in the early '70s; she became friends with photographer Steven Meisel and worked with him as a stylist on his first shoot for

the Italian magazine, *Lei*. She left Parsons to work for the junior sportswear company Bobbie Brooks, but went out on her own in 1980. She presented her first runway show in 1991, a mix of plaid ensembles (complete with matching shoes, caps, and handbags), brightly colored vinyl jackets, groovy jumpers and coats that recalled the '60s Wet Look. For some time, Sui vacillated between becoming a stylist and a designer. But with her offbeat aesthetic—one that views the world as a huge flea market—and her way of putting it all together, she is a brilliant combination of both

Avenue, and when Sybilla was a child there were always seamstresses around the house. When she was seven her family moved to Madrid, a city that would become her spiritual home. "Spain is a passionate and sensual country, full of fun. People are not especially formal; it really matters more what you are than what you look like." At sixteen, she went to Paris where she apprenticed at Saint Laurent. Ill-suited to the airs of French fashion, she returned home and began making clothes for her friends. She presented her first collection in 1983. As Sybilla became better known her clothes became less introverted: elegant coats and dresses done up in multiple yards of draped and folded fabric or given sculptural dimensions with wire hems. "I've tried to mix different aspects that seem incompatible: sensuality and sobriety, extravagance and subtlety, humor and elegance, surprise and discretion, industry and craftsmanship," she says. Sybilla has since scaled back to a couple of lines produced in Japan and a small store in Madrid. "I do different things now—objects, furniture, ballets, gardens," she says. "I'm not in the fashion world anymore, but I was never really in it."

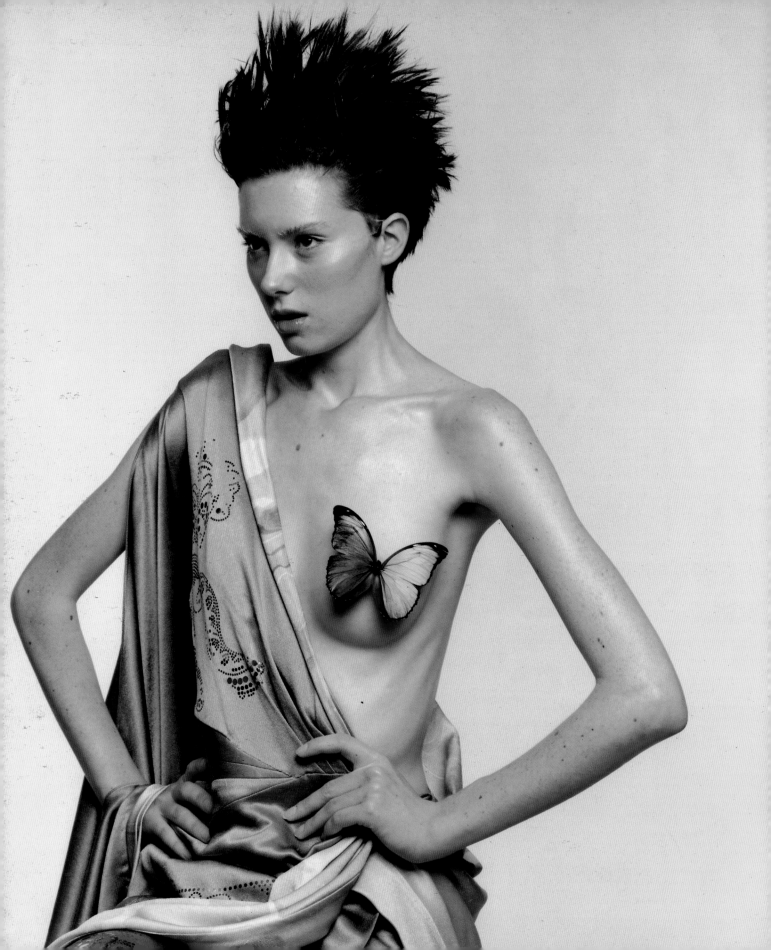

the age of eighteen it was not in search of his big fashion break but of borderline junk antiques (Tatsuno had been supporting himself doing odd jobs since he was fourteen, and selling furniture was one of them). Lacking money for clothes, he made his own. He was wearing a shirt he had cut from an antique kimono the day a buyer from Browns stopped him on the street and placed an order for thirty. With no prior experience, Tatsuno went on to cut a path through the highly established, highly elitist English made-to-measure business, opening Culture Shock with Jeannie MacArthur and Yrzuru Koga in 1983 and then, with the backing of Yohji Yamamoto, his own bespoke operation in 1987. In 1990, Tatsuno launched a collection, a mix of ready-to-wear and one-of-a-kind pieces that had little to do with his tailored past. Tatsuno designs from a state of nature: he doesn't use patterns, preferring to coax a natural shape out of fabric draped on a form, and to this day, he still cannot draw. "I'd like to think my signature is timeless individuality," he says, "each piece created by hand and unique in its own right paying little heed to the flotsam and jetsam of the fashion tide."

Ours is not a hat era. If a hat, by modern day standards, is a senseless bit of fashion finery, then Philip Treacy's hats are quite possibly insane: wild-eyed creatures that take off from the head at startling angles in a tangle of feathers or that spread their gilded wings in a sweeping arc of frothy mesh. A Treacy hat can be monumental in size and scope, like a nineteenth-century crinoline, or unobtrusive, like a single feather stuck, just so, into the hair. It can come in the shape of an exaggerated screaming violet fedora (and yes, the image of a certain character from *Alice in Wonderland*

TREACY (cont.)
Photographed by Inez van Lamsweerde & Vinoodh Matadin

has an imposing shoulder line, a subtle hourglass shape (more like half an hour, really), it weighs in at about forty-eight ounces, its insides are all handpicked, the underbelly of its collar is a work of rt, its buttonholes are so perfectly aligned and meticulously finished they could make you weep… is one hell of a jacket, and Richard Tyler *owns* it. "Simple clothing made beautifully" was how yler described his work in 1993. "I'm basically a suitmaker." A look into Tyler's fashion past, owever, reveals a lot of Lycra and sequins. The son of a costumer, Tyler came to Hollywood from

Melbourne via the rock-n-roll tour circuit. There, he spent more years than he'd like to remember creating costumes for musicians and the movies. All that glitz was enough to make Tyler want to give up fashion altogether. And in fact, he almost did. But then in 1987, Tyler met Lisa Trafficante, who became his business partner and later his wife, and together they opened the Tyler Trafficante boutique where Tyler's smart, Savile Row–inspired menswear caught the fancy of the Hollywood set—male and female alike. (Female customers kept coming into the store and asking to have

Tyler's men's suits altered to fit them.) In 1989, Tyler introduced a line of women's wear and four years later, at the age of forty-six he stood up to accept the CFDA award for best new design talent. With the launch of the Richard Tyler Couture line in March of 1997—a high-glamour collection that spotlighted Tyler's softer side as well as his burgeoning talents as a dress and eveningwear designer—Tyler's meteoric rise from tailor-to-the-stars to fashion-star in his own right is very nearly complete. But as his jackets so beautifully testify, the title of suitmaker is one that still fits him best.

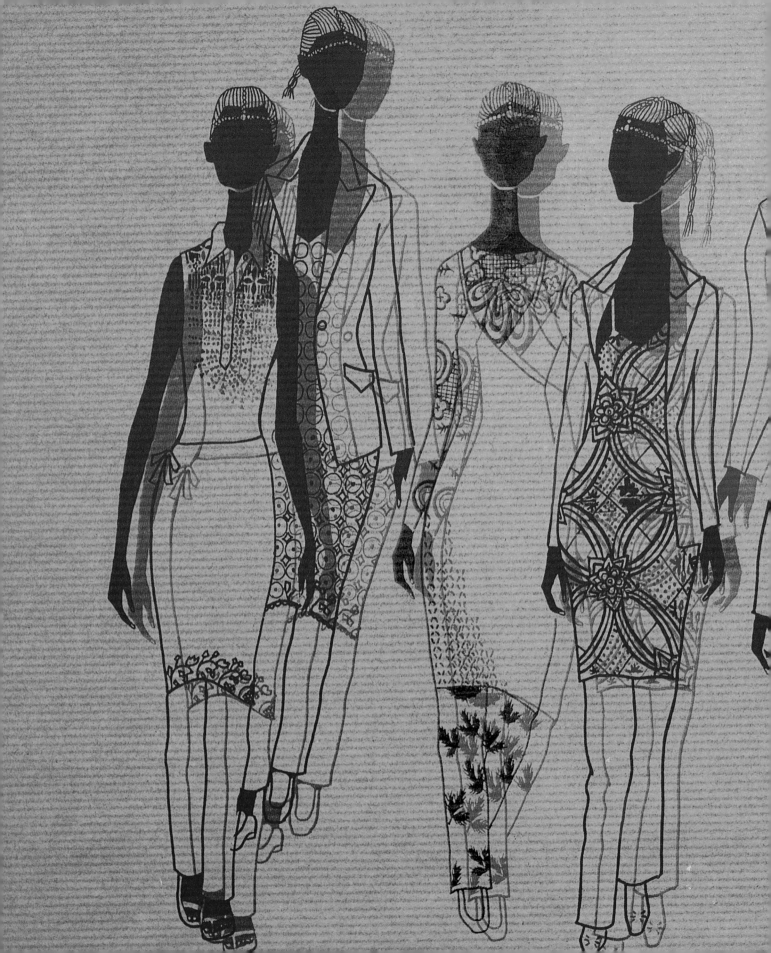

Gianni Versace was always a crowd pleaser. There is no other designer who announced Fashion!
to the world the way Versace did—perhaps because his style tended to be loud. He was unsur-
passed in his use of flashy metal mesh, tough-edged leather, pyrotechnic beading, bright colors,
eye-popping prints, and daring cuts that blare sex and rock-n-roll, the volume turned up to
eleven. But to his great credit—and to his even greater fashion fame—the art of subtlety is one
he never bothered to master. "I am working . . . I am screaming . . . to try to take women and men

VC030110A COAT 100% WOOL

VJ03002 0A JACKET 100% RAYON

VJ030090C JACKET 98% WOOL 2% POLYESTER

VS030070A SKIRT 100% WOOL

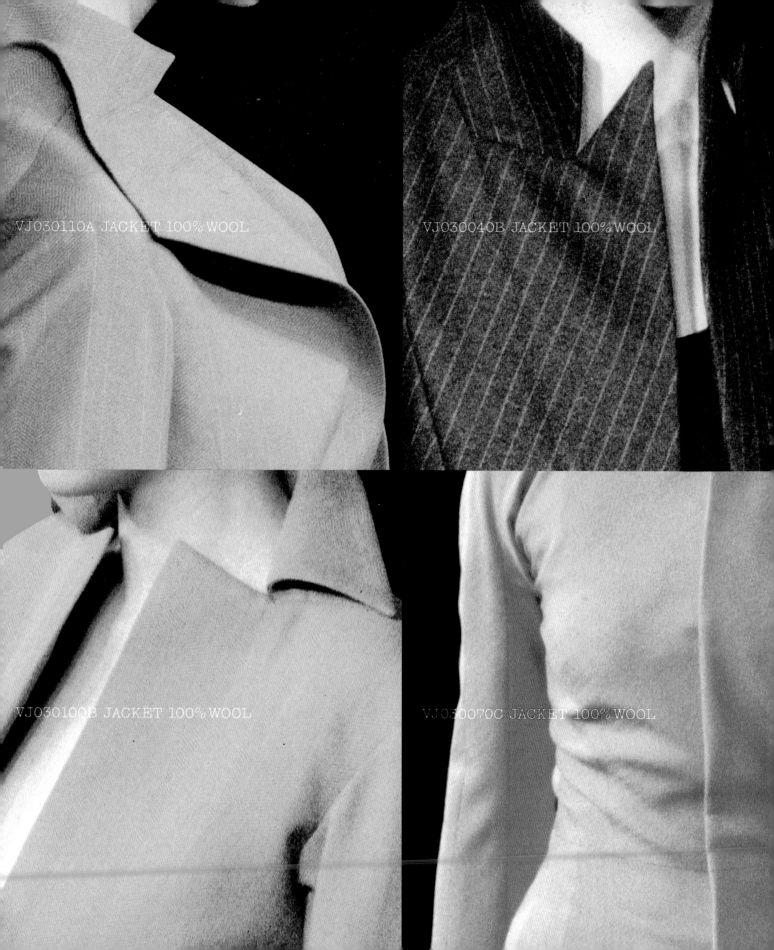

VJ030110A JACKET 100% WOOL

VJ030040B JACKET 100% WOOL

VJ030100B JACKET 100% WOOL

VJ030070C JACKET 100% WOOL